Zen Fishing and
Other Southern Pleasures

Zen Fishing and Other Southern Pleasures

Dorothy K. Fletcher

Ocean Publishing
Flagler Beach, Florida

Zen Fishing and Other Southern Pleasures

Published by:
Ocean Publishing
Post Office Box 1080
Flagler Beach, FL 32136-1080
orders@ocean-publishing.com
www.ocean-publishing.com

Cover photograph by Will Dickie

Zen Fishing artwork by Casey Scott Fletcher

ISBN, print edition   0-9767291-1-3

Library of Congress Control Number   2005925811

Printed and bound in the United States of America

Foreword

To be a poet is to peel open your soul, drink in the universe, soak up the insignificant--as well as extraordinary--moments of life, then feed that sensory amalgam back to the world through a sieve lined with curiosity, honesty, and passion.

To read poetry is to celebrate the pedestrian, to savor introspection, to revel in nuance, to be hungry for truth.

We are a rare breed, we lovers of poetry. We are eager, loyal, and ever hopeful as we digest forestfuls of diatribe, angst, and pap en route to edification. Good poetry is infinitely less abundant than bad, but when we find it, we are redeemed.

Zen Fishing & Other Southern Pleasures is good poetry. It is poetry that makes me weep, ponder, sigh, and laugh out loud. It is poetry that has captured Florida, love, loss, and the hundred-and-one ordinary things that, occasionally, make our mundane lives magical. Dottie's snapshots of everyday read like a family scrapbook: a beloved pet here, a favorite aunt there, the day the cousins went berry-picking, the night the hunting hounds bayed under the stars--simple memories that resonate in their singular focus. But it is that focused simplicity that gives these words their power. "Gather Ye Rosebuds" will haunt you. "Women I Have Loved" will make you miss maternal arms that held you close. "Beach Reverie" will make you yearn for an ocean breeze. And like the kiss whose imprint lingers on the kitchen window long after the lips have gone, Dorothy Fletcher's words will linger in your mind long after you've finished reading.

Jayne Jaudon Ferrer
Author of *Dancing with my Daughter,*
A New Mother's Prayers and
A Mother of Sons

Table of Contents

Zen Fishing

Zen Fishing

In the gentle stillness of reflection, I often come to thoughts of Zen fishing—a meditation so ancient and so satisfying that it enfolds me in deep joy and happiness. I experience Zen fishing best when my family vacations one week a year at the edge of this great continent in a cabin on the beach. Here, where there are magnificent sunrises and gentle ocean sounds—here, where terrible and powerful thunderstorms roll dramatically over our heads and out to sea, and here, where numerous lazy moments fill our hours—I can push my worries to the farthest corner of my mind as I engage in this beautiful Zen-like experience.

I learned the art from a sage friend of mine, Bill Basney. He lured me to the experience some vacations ago. I watched him as hour after hour he patiently surf-fished the Coke-bottle green waters near our vacation home. It was serenity I saw spread across his face as he expertly baited his hook, cast his line, and hooked fish after fish each and every day of our vacation. When he noticed my obvious interest and curiosity, he invited me to use one of his poles and let me begin to know the feel and the calming effects this activity produced. Soon I was hooked.

It wasn't long before my husband, Hardy, and I owned our own Shakespeare "Ugly Stiks"™ along with tackle box with reel holders. Now, we make quite a pair as we brave the elements and harvest the bounty of the sea.

In a most disciplined pattern, we now begin our meditation by properly preparing for the experience. We carry our cooler, rods and reels, and bait down to the edge of the rolling morning waves. The sun joins us, first in a golden display, and then, it eventually glitters like quicksilver on the surface of the water. Breezes come gently and sandpipers teeter back and forth waiting for us to discard shrimp heads and tails as we bait our hooks. Grackles gather to watch our dancing. Covered in sunblock, hats and t-shirts, we move, side by side, enjoying each other and the Zen-like quality of the fishing meditation.

First, comes the cast. Then there's the tightening of the line. Waiting follows. Often a great deal of waiting has to happen. Slowly, we reel the line in and then BAM! There's a hit! You know in your soul something has taken the bait. It is a wild, life struggle you can actually feel at the end of your rig as the fish darts and dodges, fighting you until it can move no more. Finally exhausted, the fish lets you pull it in, pull the hook out, and throw it into ice where it heaves its last and lets you have its body to eat.

One extraordinary day we caught twenty slithering, silvery whiting. By nightfall I had cleaned, battered, fried and then served the fish with grits and coleslaw as if I were some kind of fishmonger's wife. Fresh fish! It was grand,

and I was absolutely and joyously exhausted by the time the dishes were washed and I trudged off to my vacation bed. All night long, my arms could feel the tug of dream fish and my heart rested in blessed oblivion.

I have to admit that there are times I feel uncomfortable about my role in this food chain. Karma says that in my next life, I'll play the fish's role. I'll be the dinner. However, I just can't let those feelings last very long. There are so many fish, so little time.

One of the best benefits of Zen fishing is the sense that that is all that I am—fishing. I am not a wife or mother or teacher. I simply am. And there are not many things in my life that can be so restful. Even as I physically exert myself, I am rested with all that casting and reeling and landing. It is a joyous, bountiful time.

I cannot wait until there is an incoming tide, the wind is from the south, and I can once again cast my line upon the water and become one with the rod.

Beach Reverie

green like jade
warm ocean waters
roll in with wild horse legs

all ajumble
galloping at the ends
of the color

diminishing in size
as they draw near
the end of the world

only to slide back
to begin the race again
I could watch this

joy forever but I
close my eyes
to absorb the sounds

of wild waves
of hungry gulls
of children playing

clean breezes wash
over warmed skin
basking in gold

I let myself melt
into beach colors
beiges and blond

like sands
my jade eyes open
my blue soul rises

running with water
horses to horizons
I can only imagine

this is my heaven

Wind Chimes

The sound usually comes to me on the soft Florida breezes, but in the spring that sound almost comes in blasts as the winds roar through the trees—my neighborhood—my wind chimes. I can't even remember who gave me my first set of wind chimes—who first set my heart soaring with the magical tinkling sound that they made—but I suspect that it was my father. I believe that he brought them home to me from Japan, a land he had visited when he was serving in the Navy in the Korean War.

Those first chimes were made of a handful of glass pieces about the size and shape of microscope slides. Each had been cheerfully decorated with red and white paint by a worker somewhere in the Orient. The pieces dangled down little strings which hung from concentric circles of red bamboo. Then we hung them from the ceiling of a corner in our screen porch.

I was truly mesmerized by the sound these little chimes made. It was such a happy sound, unless, of course, a thunderstorm threatened. Then the sound became a little hysterical, and I worried that they might disintegrate on the spot. They never did, though, until we moved. Then they mysteriously went the way of all "things lost" during great migrations.

When we moved to Florida, I discovered a new kind of wind chime, a creation made of beach shells. These chimes were usually fashioned with strings of mollusk shells suspended from an interesting piece of driftwood. I would like to think that the natives indigenous to Florida made these chimes, but more than likely they too were made in Japan.

Although these chimes did not produce the same sound as my first set, the soft music they played was still delightful. They were cheerful in timbre and tone, and their earth colors and origins made for a Sixties kind of back-to-Mother-Earth mentality that I was beginning to espouse back in those days. Whatever happened to these chimes, I don't remember. More than likely they are in a box in the attic along with my bell-bottoms and dashiki shirt and are best left to the past.

My most recent set of wind chimes was made of metal pipes of varying lengths. Supposedly, these pipes were carefully designed by Buddhist monks to create tones that are soothing to the soul. Since I got this set of chimes at Ace Hardware, I seriously doubt my soul was a factor in their design. I have to admit, though, that listening to them sing in the breeze while I sip my iced tea in the summer or a mug of hot cocoa in the winter has been most soothing to my sensibilities.

Of course, I probably am one of those obnoxious neighbors that Ann Landers' readers write about, ones who keep the neighbors up all night with their eccentricities—like wind chimes. What I have noticed about the chimes that hang right outside of my bedroom window is that they have just become a part of the sounds of life out there. They have become like a mantle clock or those grandfather clocks that chime every hour on the hour. At first they keep the family up all night with their noise, but then, as time passes, they become part of the surroundings. Unless a person makes an effort to hear them, he or she usually doesn't.

I guess it is my soul that listens to the chimes now. My conscious self rarely hears them anymore, except when the wind really kicks up. Then I am flooded with a variety of wonderful impressions that will surely make me see to it that wind chimes hang always in the corners of my life.

Mimosa Breezes/ Ft. Worth, Texas

some lullabies
cannot be heard
are carried on breezes
settle like silent

mimosa pollen
on window sills
then with a sweep
of an oscillating fan

or the movement
of a gentle thought
across the room
a soft scent scatters

and Bluebonnet Circle
sparkles again
in hot summer nights
costume gaudy

green   yellow   neon
signs on the prairie
shimmering through windows
drug store   five and dime

Maude's Cafe
liven up dark neighborhoods
glitter in sleepy eyes
like rhinestone rings

on Mama's dresser
falling asleep on Papa's
shoulder so solid
like thick mimosa

branches that waited
outside for morning
for little girls to climb
settle in pink branches

breathe in memories
that quicken even now
whenever the wind blows
and mimosa trees blossom

The Great Snow of '57

It began during a mathematics lesson in Miss Milling's second grade class at Hyde Park Elementary in 1957. We were reciting our "number families" aloud when suddenly Miss Milling looked up from her book and out the window. "Oh, my God!" she breathed.

All thirty little heads turned in the direction she was looking and saw the big, lacy, white flakes floating down and filling the little courtyard just beyond our classroom window. That's when pandemonium broke out. Chairs were knocked over; tables were knocked askew; one child was even knocked to the floor in the mad rush of excited seven-year-olds to the window side of the room. All except me, of course. I was the new kid who had just moved to Florida from East St. Louis, Illinois, three months prior, and snow was hardly a thing to amaze.

Oh, sure, snow had its wonders. That first snowfall was always a treat, and snow on Saturday was the best. Saturday snow could be played in until your snowsuit was drenched with moisture and your hands were frozen to the mittens. After a while, however, snow lost its charm and became something to be overcome and trudged through. By the end of winter it was a slushy, unsightly mush.

Snow was one of the things my family was trying to avoid when we came to Florida. When my dad's company transferred him to Jacksonville, we thought we had died and gone to heaven. I thought I'd get to bury my snowsuit and mittens for good. I was told that I'd be picking my breakfast off orange trees in the backyard. I could catch my lunch and dinner in the nearby ocean and wash them down with coconut milk from the local palms. The winters, we were told, were so mild that we didn't even need a furnace — a space heater would do very nicely.

I was thinking about that utterly inadequate heater as those large flakes came and danced around my new, happy friends. I watched in amazement as the giddy children of my class ran outside in shirtsleeves and frolicked in the cold. They were nuts, I thought, not realizing that this was probably the first time any of these children had ever seen snow. Why, it was probably the first time Miss Milling had ever seen snow, because she was out there in the midst of all the hoopla.

"Hey," Johnny Roberts yelled as he came running in to get me, "it's snowing out here!"

"I know," I replied. "I know."

And I did know. I remembered how, on the frosty night before, my visiting grandfather sat on our sofa in the middle of the night. He was dressed in his overcoat. He was sporting his fedora, and he was cussing up a storm about how cold he was and how lousy Florida actually was. In the meantime, my mother tucked us children under all the blankets we owned. She even used beach towels on top of that, lest we freeze to death in our Florida paradise.

When my family actually survived that winter, the first thing my father did was buy a house with a furnace. He wouldn't even look at houses with space heaters. And we have been snug ever since. Not all of our Florida dreams have come true, however. We have never eaten a fresh-picked orange breakfast and only rarely caught enough fish to make a meal. And as far as I know, there are no coconut palms around here, but still we've stayed.

And when people complain that the heat and humidity are getting to them and how they can't wait for winter, I just remember the winter of 1957. Then, I let the perspiration glisten as I soak in all the heat I can find.

Barefoot

some time in May
almost to June
long after daffodils
have faded and shriveled

my mama would say
come take off those shoes, Child
and I'd smile so big
my hot little feet

free of their winter
binding of leather and cotton
couldn't wait to sink
languidly down into cool

blades of green grass
of weeds so soft
so refreshing
I tickled with dances

sped over yards
in little girl races
pranced so quickly to orchards
fine snowless meadows

by nightfall I'd have marched
a hundred happy miles
calluses beginning
on my summer soles

and dirty   my yes
you could grow corn
between your toes
mama would laugh

as she scrubbed
using a sponge
born without any feet
at all   in my dream

I need no shoes
all journeys are shoeless
my world carpeted
in purest summer memory

Mountains, Memory, and Marguerite

All summer memories are special in my mind, but I have a series of memories that take me back to one extraordinary summer. It was the summer when Marguerite Dovi and I were just ten years old. We were spindly legged, flat-chested, and the very best of friends. One special moment has us making blackberry jam from the blackberries we picked in a pasture on top of a mountain in Boone, North Carolina. The second vivid recollection is of us playing in an icy mountain stream, and the last is of a night spent under the stars on top of a mountain.

In the first memory, I can see Marguerite, my mother, and me in the pine-paneled kitchen of our cabin as blackberries began a rolling boil in a large pot on top of an efficiency stove. A heavenly aroma swirled about us in the heat our cooking produced. Lush mountain scenery beckoned from the window near the sink as cleaned and boiled jars lined the counter, ready for us to preserve our wonderful summer day for winter breakfasts. Since that moment, I have never looked at a blackberry in the same way. Not only is it a fruit to be savored, but it has also become a symbol to me of a mythical time and place.

In a second flash of memory, I can see Marguerite and me straddling a little brook in the valley beneath the cabin we rented. The cheerful sounding water cut through the forest greenery of magnificent and towering trees as shafts of sunlight cut through the canopy formed by the leaves. The water we played in was crystal clear and colder than the water stored in refrigerators. We built little dams with the rounded, smooth stones that had lined the banks. For hours we pretended that we were both Joan of Arcs holding back the armies of the Burgundians with our flights of fancy.

I recall the magic of all our nights spent in North Carolina, where it was cool in the summer and blankets had to be dug out of the cedar chest even in July and August; but the night we spent on top of the mountain was truly the highlight of the whole trip and the memory I most treasure.

Marguerite and I lugged up the mountain our Girl Scout regulation bedrolls made out of sheets and numerous quilts. We then carefully spread them out in the same green pasture where we had collected our blackberries. Here we snuggled up against the cool darkness under the stars. We were from the big metropolis of Jacksonville, Florida, a city that was in the process of lining all the streets with street lamps in the late Fifties. We girls were awestruck by the number and the brilliance of stars that could be seen when you weren't near a city. We could actually see that there was a Milky Way—a ghostly, cloud-like wisp that traversed the sky, looking like a great path for Orion to walk. We also caught glimpses of at least a dozen shooting stars that whizzed past us as the night crept toward morning.

I recall that there was a group of local hunters nearby with a campfire blazing. We could hear them telling stories as we all listened to the baying of their hounds on the trail of raccoon or opossum. Marguerite and I talked late into the night, too. We confided all our secrets about boyfriends, imagined or real, and visualized what our husbands would be like. The night passed too quickly.

Before we knew it, we were facing the golden dawn with its incredible brightness and the damp covers that our bedrolls had become as the dew had settled in the night. Adolescence also loomed on our horizon, and soon we would be too "mature" for such magical times. This would be our last summer together.

Soon we were all packed up and crammed into the family Ford heading home to Florida, the mundane, and the process of growing up and older. And yet, the glory of that summer comes to life for me every time blackberries are in season, every time I cross a stream in my travels, or any time I look into a magnificent night sky.

Starry Night

we slept in pastures
on a mountain
once   under sky

Carolina hunters sat
near us   around a fire
passing a jug

listening
to their baying hounds
on the trail of raccoon

they didn't bother us
we could hardly hear
their bawdy talk

but lonesome howls
of their hunting hounds
echoed through the valley

drowning out
any death cries
raccoon might have made

when the sun came up
filling the mist
with blood red light

the men were gone
they'd stumbled home
when the fires went out

lean silhouetted hounds
nosed at our blankets
with bloody snouts

then snuffled away
when we proved
an unfamiliar scent

Morning

For many years it has been my custom to awaken long before I have to go to work, so that I can sit in the morning quiet and come to terms with the day. In the winter I sit snuggled on my sofa and drink my coffee in the dark, meditating on what has and what will happen to me at my job. In the spring, the summer, and the fall, when the weather and mosquitoes permit, I sit with my coffee at an old wooden picnic table on my backyard deck and watch the world come to life.

Mornings have always held certain magic for me. The majesty of the sunrise is truly a wonder to behold. When there are no clouds, the sky slowly changes from black to dark purple to lavender to pink and then to daylight. When there are large banks of clouds, all the color shifts are accompanied by rays of light piercing the fluff and heralding the day. When there is an overcast sky, the changes are merely from black to gray to white.

Day after day, with no prompting from us humans, the morning comes. Day after day you can find me up before the sun, watching and preparing for its arrival.

One summer morning was particularly magnificent. I sat at the picnic table and sipped my coffee, carefully coming to consciousness. My three cats were near, stretching and yawning after a long night of mousing. Bosco, the biggest, washed his face and whiskers. Jones, the white one, stood out against the fading night. I could barely make out Kitty, my tortoiseshell cat.

The morning stars overhead were still very bright, because I could still make them out without my glasses on. I could see the constellation, Orion, as he stood proudly over the tree shadows that surrounded me, their lacy silhouettes against the brightening sky.

Then, out of the huge dark shadow that was my neighbor's tree, a large mass of darkness suddenly erupted from the shadow's edge. Slowly the mass unfolded into the shape of a great bird with a considerable wingspan. As my cats and I sat there in awed silence, we watched as the shape grew larger and larger, coming closer and closer.

I don't know if it were real or if I had imagined it. The hour was, after all, quite early. I could have been dreaming, I suppose; but I could have sworn that as the creature passed just a few feet over my head, I felt the turbulence of its wings upon my upturned face. I could tell that I was being carefully observed and analyzed. And when the flying animal had made sure that I was neither food nor anything with which he'd care to tangle, his shadow was absorbed into the darkness on the opposite side of my yard. It was glorious.

I'm not sure what the significance of this event was. Were I a Native American I might have ascribed a meaning to the shadow; it was an omen or a portent for the future. My modern day self thought this "sign" to be a good one. After all, it had lifted my spirits. I had witnessed something rare and beautiful.

Later, as I stood at the counter in my kitchen pouring cat crunchies into three bowls, the sound of a hoot owl calling came gently to me from far in the distance. It was going to be a good day.

Bedding the Birds

When I first moved to Jacksonville, Florida, in the late Fifties, back when the city limits went only in a five-mile radius instead of all the way to the county line, there was so much lush forest, so many virgin swamps and fertile pastures, that I felt as if we had moved far into the country. I felt rather like Jody, from The Yearling, as I explored the woods just beyond my neighborhood hoping to see deer that were indigenous to the area. Of course, we children were much too loud in our journeys to have made that possible, but still we would catch glimpses of squirrels and raccoons and snakes on occasion.

As progress marched through the area, I sadly watched as one parcel of land after another made way for a strip mall or parking lot, until finally I felt like I was in the middle of the proverbial "asphalt jungle." As a young woman, I protested the overzealous building rampage by voting for environmentally sensitive types and by supporting those organizations that seemed to care about God's little creatures, no matter how small and seemingly unimportant. I passed my caring spirit on to my children, hoping that they would learn to conserve our precious resources, to recycle, and to vote responsibly.

While I was doing all of this, I became aware very slowly that maybe man is not as powerful as he might think. When the forests went away, raccoons moved into our backyards and found a ready supply of food in our garbage cans and refuse piles. Opossum began to move into our shrubbery and nightly raided the cat dishes we left on our stoop for our kitties. Seagulls have learned that parking lots resemble bodies of water from the air and that they often contain discarded french fries and hamburger remnants that are far easier to catch than fish. Even the little brown sparrows, which were displaced when their homes were bulldozed, simply took up residence in the crooks of the big letters of the Publix and Albertson's supermarket signs. Here they stay warmer in winter than in any tree, and there is the ready supply of discarded human things from which to make their nests and to provide their chicks with food.

I feel a tremendous comfort in all of this, especially at sundown, when I go to the store for some special ingredient for supper and find all the little birds chattering away as they prepare for the night. It seems as if hundreds of them descend upon my nearest grocery store and take up their perches in the ornamental shrubs or in the P's, U's and O's of the illuminated letters. Like the swallows that go to Capistrano, these busy birds swarm down upon the manmade landscape and adapt. Maybe there is hope for us after all.

The Nature of the Beast

the sound of frantic
dying birds wings
comes from the window sill

I look up and see
my sleeping cat
sunning himself
near the marmalade jars
that match his color

feathers tangle
in his whiskers
dreams move
across closed eyes

soft   silent   stalking
hard cries of capture
bloody warm calm

I recognize the sound
in the roaring
of his purr

Key West Cats

In my thirty-three-year career as an English teacher, I have been fortunate to earn my living by reading and teaching the works of the best authors ever to have written in the English language. However, before I even knew how to read, I have loved cats. So, when I was able to combine two passions of mine during a week's vacation to Key West, Florida, I can only tell you that I was in heaven.

Visiting the home of Ernest Hemingway, one of my favorite American authors, was like fulfilling a lifelong dream. His beautiful two-storied, limestone house is located on the corner of Whitehead Street and Olivia Street. Not only was the location one of the most lush, green settings I have ever encountered, but it is also the place where Hemingway wrote many of his most important novels. The olive green building forming the estate's main living quarters has two wonderful verandas that encircle both levels. Tropical trees of every kind enfold the house and carefully tended gardens are all over the compound. All throughout the premises, tourists get many glimpses of the dozens of cats that are allowed to roam free on the grounds.

The home where these felines live is the only house in the Keys with a basement from which the limestone to build the house was quarried. This space made a very good wine cellar that Hemingway kept well stocked. This house is also the first house in Key West to have a built-in, saltwater swimming pool, where the cats may sometimes be seen drinking. Rainwater is not as heavy as saltwater and accumulates on the top.

What is most interesting about the cats that live here is that they are all descended from one cat, Snowball, who had been a gift to the author from a ship's captain. We know that all the cats on the compound are direct descendants because the original Snowball was polydactyl or had six toes on each paw.

On the lovely morning when I went to visit the Hemingway House Museum, the weather was a little on the brisk side. It was all of 65 degrees, quite cool by Key West standards. I had ridden my rented bicycle there—a most appropriate way to travel in the Keys—and paid my $9 to get into the museum. Immediately, a solid black, six-toed male cat approached me and began rubbing up against my shin even as I put my bike in the rack.

I could hardly step anywhere after that I didn't come close to stepping on some big-named feline. There was "Lana Turner," "Sandra Bullock," and the misunderstood "Mr. Bette Davis." One of the most arrogant and beautiful creatures on the property is "Archibald MacLeish." Archibald, an orange tabby, with tremendous, six-toed paws, is featured in the museum's brochure. On the day I was at the museum, he had spread his full length across an Oriental rug and those of us on the tour had to step over him as we progressed through the bright and airy parlor.

After I spent an informative time on the guided tour, I strolled through the gardens of the estate imagining what it must have been like to live here. How could anyone NOT be inspired in this setting? Cats pranced and cavorted everywhere I walked. Eventually, I took a seat in the sun and proceeded to write in my journal about all the remarkable feelings this literary place produced in me. As I did so, a very demure calico walked over to my chair and then sprang into my lap. Before I could stop my pen, the cat had made herself at home. She kneaded my thighs for a moment, and then—purring loudly—my little visitor curled up and went to sleep in my lap as if we were old friends. I stroked her soft, silky fur as she slept, and soon realized that she had six toes. At that moment I felt connected to a real literary presence that permeated the place. After all, here I was holding a descendant of Snowball, a cat I know Ernest himself must have stroked and loved, maybe in the very spot where I was sitting.

I worried for a little while that the curator or tour guide might come and chastise me for "holding" a cat, but soon I relaxed when I realized that no one was going to break up this happy moment. I stayed with my little calico for well over an hour, and what a delightful time it was! The sun was warm, the scenery was breathtakingly beautiful, and the company was excellent.

I never caught her name, my little calico—but I took her picture before I left. She eventually moved on to another garden chair when the shadows began to grow long, and it was getting close to feeding time. As she moved away from me, I couldn't help but notice that her six-toed paws resembled tiny hands. It was a marvel! I consider myself most fortunate to have had such a warm fuzzy memory by which to remember my time in Key West.

Thanksgiving at Ernest Hemingway's
Key West, Florida, 2000

we sit on sunny verandas
framed by lush green
smoking our fat, sweet cigars
and commenting on the cats

one takes to me and crawls up
into my lap as smoke envelops
our conversation
about life lived so intensely
that we couldn't bear
it all the way to its end

and the breeze rattles
the fronds of palms
and the cat purrs
under my hand

and a thousand satisfactions
rest in my heart
as Ernest puffs away, smiling

Encountering the Feminine

Encountering the Feminine

I got to know
Great-grandmother
by reading family photographs

her old and faded images
were tall and wearing
cotton dresses
gentle faces

she was in the background
always
but she was always there
my mother's reverent voices

told me over
and over the years
my great-grandmother
became a presence

as soft as Amazing Grace
sung on a distant
Sunday morning

Mama's House

my mama's house
has childless rooms
quiet halls

she's filled her emptiness
with furniture and plush decor
from magazines

soft pastel colors
coat all her walls like icing
that little kids
would love to lick

her overstuffed sofa
sits like a fat lady's lap
ready for stories
soft and inviting

delicate vases grace
high polished tables
instead of the jelly jars
we used to use

silk flowers blossom now
instead of child-harvest weeds
by the fistful

only ghosts of memory remain
hidden and sought
behind cleaned chairs
and always closed closets

and Mama has become
a ghost as well
only rarely seen
in her house anymore
enjoying the beauty of things
she had once imagined
important

Mama's Garden

Sometimes I feel as if my own mother is Mother Nature herself. In her garden, lush, green growth spills over pots and beds and troughs. Shady trees soften the effects of the summer sun as cats peek out of their hiding places. Birds visit the feeders as little stone girls play and stone turtles crawl through thick flowers. The air is sweet and carries the scent of the many herb beds that flourish there. Rocks and stones accent corners and soften the lines the edger has carved in the grass. Buddha smiles from his stone pedestal.

The outer rim of the yard is lined with trees—some oak, some pine, all large and shady. The wooden privacy fence holds hanging pots of ivy, which droop over the edges and hang down to touch the rising stalks of day lilies, herb dishes, morning glory vines and rounded mounds of impatiens. There is then a thick line of dark green border grass, which seems to hold the explosion of flowers within its boundary. Then comes a thick layer of light green grass, which holds in it an orange tree and a gardenia bush. This brings us to the garden spot just in front of the patio where rose bushes sprout and blossom with fat, fist-sized roses of red and pink and yellow. Sweet basil, catnip, parsley and mint scent the air with their sweetness. More impatiens color the landscape.

In the stillness this haven creates, wind chimes softly sing their melodies on the breath of God wind that swirls gently there. Birds join the chorus—especially the cardinals who have a nest somewhere near. Pines whisper and Sinbad, Mama's fattest cat, purrs contently on the warm patio where he spends his day.

Anyone who could grow such a place must have some sort of magic in her touch. I believe and have believed for a very long time that my mother is such a woman. Her garden is so vibrant and alive and beautiful—only one with very special gifts could make such a place happen. I know this when I see her out in the sun, a straw bonnet on her head, long skirt on her body, and long-handled hoe in her hands. I can also see it in her as she sits in a lawn chair reading some book and drinking a glass of iced tea in the evening. She and her garden are most remarkable.

Eve's Garden

she poured strong tea
into fine china cups

directed my eyes
to pansies

in the yard
beyond windows

new green and tulips
crocus and daffodils

stand out
in sunshine

softly Eve talked
about her dogwood

blossoms exploding
thick on heavy branches

she'd planted the tree
right

on the spot
where her little boy

was found dead
long, long ago

did I want any sugar
maybe lemon or honey

Chess Pie and Neenie

When warm weather comes and fills my windows with sweet smells of spring, I am reminded of the wonderful visits my paternal grandmother, Neenie (a great-uncle's corruption of Irene), made to our house in Florida. With her she brought the knowledge of many wonderful recipes, but the most delectable that I have ever let pass my lips was her Chess Pie.

She told me all about it as I stood with little-girl elbows on the counter watching her as she prepared it. When the weather warmed up in Tennessee where she had grown up, it was necessary to use up all the perishables that were stored in the springhouse. Butter and eggs were the primary ingredients, but sugar was also used in large quantities. Eventually there would be fifteen or more pies to be sold or given as gifts.

There is a story about how the name was derived—about how a Yankee newspaper reporter had misunderstood the Southern accent. He thought "chess" was what the Southerner had called this dish, when in fact the cook had called it "just" pie, meaning a pie without any fruit.

I would recall that story each time Neenie would remove the golden treasure from the oven, filling the kitchen with a heavenly aroma that actually made my mouth water. It was all I could do to wait for the pie to cool off so that I could eat my fill and roll my eyes with delight.

Neenie's Chess Pie Recipe

Preheat oven to 350.

> 1 unbaked pie shell
> ½ cup of butter or margarine
> 1 cup sugar
> 3 beaten eggs
> 1 Tbs vinegar
> 1 Tbs cornmeal
> 1 teaspoon vanilla

Cream the butter with a fork, gradually adding the sugar. Add the eggs, vinegar, cornmeal and vanilla. Mix until well blended. Pour into pie shell. Bake at 350 for about 1 hour. (Be sure to check on it the last 15 minutes. If it appears too brown, lower heat to 300 for the remaining minutes). Allow to cool and then serve. Keep remaining pie refrigerated. Tastes great cold.

Lady Food

she wouldn't dream of serving
sandwiches with crusts
her crabapple slices were
properly chilled and fanned

out on finest china plates
iced tea swirled cubes
of crystal ice tinkling
in lemoned glasses

cream cheese softened
slowly on sweet nut bread
finally she scooped
mounds of chicken salad

heaped with walnuts, grapes
finely chopped parsley
after grace was said and sugar
spread on strawberries bobbing

in bowls of heavy cream
we little girls in pretty dresses
lined our laps with linen
and ate with petite bites

every morsel Grandmama
had made for us with love

Hard Journeys and Relationships

I think it was Olivia Dukakis who said it best in Steel Magnolias. "That which does not kill us makes us strong." That line keeps coming to me as I put my vacation photos in an album, and my mother-in-law, Betty, lies in her bed as ill as she has ever been. She apparently caught the flu when the two of us were in England and France last week. This was to have been the trip of a lifetime for us—I, an English major who wanted just to wander the streets of London and use my high school French in Paris, and she, an avid reader who wanted only to see the wide world for the first time.

Our first mistake was joining a tour group designed for teenagers. I thought that educational tours had very reasonable prices, and the sights provided would be the most popular ones. I was right about those things. What I hadn't counted on was the incredible energy level that would be required to keep up with the group. Neither Betty nor I was ready for that.

Ours was a whirlwind tour of London and Paris, which was to cover seven days. I had overestimated what could be done in that short time when I was looking at travel brochures. Every picture made me want to cram in just one more outing, and the human body can only do so much in an allotted amount of time. It's a matter of physics.

Aside from air turbulence and general motion sickness, which often accompany any trip, there were two major disappointments. The British Museum's Library—a place in which I wanted to spend an afternoon checking out the original manuscripts of Shakespeare, Brontë, Handel, and other masters—had been moved to a new location and was not yet open to the public. Then, in our mad rush to catch the ferry to Calais, we had less than an hour to walk one mile to Canterbury Cathedral and back. Betty had to pass, and even I was only able to stare at the outside of a building where millions of pilgrims had prayed over 1,400 years.

There were high points, though. We got to see *Miss Saigon* in the Drury Lane Theatre, one of the oldest continuously operating theatres in England. Still in the back of my mind I worried about having to hail a taxi in the dark in this foreign country, which took a bit out of the enjoyment of the musical for me. We made it to the hotel safely, but for a while I had been afraid that we might be forever stuck in the theatre district of London.

Then there was the morning I discovered the Dickens Museum. For £2.50, I got to see where this writer lived and worked. Hoping that some of his genius might rub off, I even touched the glass case wherein his desk was kept.

Another wonder was Windsor Castle. Since there was a three-story flight of stairs to get into the place and no elevator to be found, Betty opted to stay beneath at the gift shop, while I went with the group into the castle grounds. Wonderfully, however, it began to snow, a rare treat for a Florida girl, but a cold one for those left waiting. I hurriedly walked through St. George's Chapel where I saw Henry the VIII's and Jane Seymour's graves, then I hurried back to where my mother-in-law waited. We took tea in a quaint little shop while the snow flurried down on the emerging spring flowers just beyond our window. It was beautiful!

France provided another set of problems, not the least of which was the cold, rainy weather and an inadequacy of elevators. Stairs loomed everywhere, from Le Louvre, which was a Stairmaster nightmare, to our tiny hotel, which had a one-man lift. Once Betty got to the room, I ventured out into the rain to go get her some provisions at the "Supermarche" across the street. As I stood at the stoplight in the drizzle, a woman came up to me and in French asked me if I wanted to share her umbrella. I thanked her in my best but broken high school French, and she escorted me across the street. No one can ever tell me that the French are a rude lot.

There were two other wonderful moments for me in Paris. One was on the Bateaux Mouche, a boat ride in the night and in the rain. I stood bundled up on the deck and marveled at the tremendous beauty of this ancient "city of lights." I was cold, to be sure, but I decided to use this chilly memory on one of those hot, Florida summer afternoons, when I get into my car and think I'm going to pass out from the heat. I'll just go back to this cold Paris night and cool off.

The other unforgettable experience was visiting Notre Dame on the Ile de la Cité. It was an emotional high point for me. As I sat in prayer in the incredible, vaulted arched nave of that cathedral, I wept. All those years of imagining what this moment would be like, and magically, I was there. It was a miracle of sorts.

As awful as parts of our traveling experience were, I really got to know my mother-in-law. We often found ourselves doubled over in laughter as we considered the absurdity of certain situations and told stories to pass the time as we rode in buses and planes. We may have been a bit punchy, but we weren't crying. And we're still friends. That says a lot about us and traveling, and if we can just get Betty well from her flu, we'll be much stronger for our time together in jolly ol' England and gay Paris.

Women I Have Loved

her scent reminded me
of limes
piled neatly in produce
but she was standing
there—in pickles/spices/
condiments aisle
checking out
the mayonnaise prices

big, brown woman
dressed in red batik patterns
with a matching kerchief
covering plaited hair
a gentle fragrance
encircled her
then me
as I passed her by

limeade summers
and shortbread songs
sang in my head
and I delighted
in her being
there

big, brown flower
sprung full grown
from the grocery floor

Sleeping with Bears

Sleeping with Bears

as long ago as I can remember
I've slept with bears
first plush teddies holding
witches/ghosts of darkness

at bay   then when grandfather
came to die filling the night
house with real growls
as he snored in the room

nearby bears prowled
my childhood dreams
hid in closets   under beds
breathing/roaring

my golden hair sticking
to my fevered head
learning life's lesson in the dark
not to pick up whip or chair

but just lay down beside
what scared me most
like a lamb with the lion
I took the beast to heart

went in and lay next to his old pain
giving him bear hugs
the monster lost his power
over me   I could stroke

his furry rage avoiding
his painful smile
it is little wonder
then that I would marry

love to death
a burly bear/man
snoring a reassuring
rhythm in my life

constant   measured
a comforting presence
for as long as

we both shall live

Mystery

He was descended from Irish immigrants who came to America when famine drove hordes of beings west to distant shores. Papa was dark and handsome in all his younger photographs. It was small wonder that my grandmother fell passionately in love with him and eloped with him at her earliest convenience.

My mother told me all about Papa as a young father— how his hugs always followed discipline when she was bad, how he took care of her pet turtles when she went to Birmingham for the summer, and how he always put a calming hand on her shoulder when her mother would lecture her "ad nauseam" about this and that.

I got to know Papa when my mother and I moved in with my grandparents while Daddy, my father, was shipped off to fight in Korea. By then Papa was not so svelte as his younger photographs, but his smile alone could put a shine on your shoes, and soon I followed Papa wherever he went.

As far as I could tell, Papa was affection incarnate. He was gentle and patient, and I can still hear his deep choir-member voice saying, "Hello, lil' dahlin'." He would let me, his first granddaughter, sit in his lap for hours, combing his hair, combing his eyebrows while listening to the Cardinals play baseball on the radio. Many a time we'd drift off to sleep in the warmth of St. Louis summer afternoons. I've seen the many photographs as proof—both of us open mouthed and probably snoring in the great armchair that dominated his living room.

I remember nights when the family would adjourn to the porch after dinner, waiting in the coolness for the day to pass into night. I would again nestle myself in Papa's arms that enveloped me as the darkness enveloped the earth. It was during one of those peaceful evening moments that I learned that there was at least one Bible story that my devotedly faithful grandfather did not believe.

"I won't believe it," Papa said, "that God would ever ask a person to kill a child, much less his own. Abraham would not have been asked to slaughter Isaac. What kind of God would ask such a thing? No God I could worship."

"Now, Fred," my grandmother chided, as her crochet needle moved briskly on the coverlet she would have ready for winter.

"Sorry, Elizabeth. My God would never ask such a thing. I am flabbergasted that it even got into the Bible in the first place."

"But, Dad," my young uncle began, "it's about obedience and doing whatever Gods demands."

"Well, I don't care," Papa said as forcefully as I ever heard him speak. "God would never demand that a man kill a child. The Bible writer must have made a mistake."

This heretical conversation thankfully ended when a brief silence followed and then a new topic arose—baseball concerns or vacation plans—I don't remember what exactly. It was just nice to have our happier voices again joining the noisy drone of the cicadas.

When Papa died ten years later, we were all horribly shaken. His death at sixty-three was premature and most unexpected. None of us was ready for the vacuum created by his leaving. At the time of Papa's death, my father had long since returned from the Korean War. My parents, a brother and two sisters and I now lived a thousand miles away from those magical summer memories with Papa.

One incident that I found profoundly telling, though, was something that occurred not too long after Papa's death. My grandmother in her grief wanted to memorialize my grandfather so she gave a considerable sum of her inheritance to the Methodist church in his name. The church took the money and ordered a magnificent stained glass window as part of their renovation project. At the unveiling, my grandmother was horrified to see Abraham in glistening, vibrant, sun-drenched color brandishing his knife over his bound son's waiting neck.

"It was horrible," my grandmother said, weeping over the phone to my mother. "Of all the countless Bible stories to choose to celebrate Fred's life, they had to pick the very one he hated the most and understood the least!"

As my mother hung up the phone and relayed the incident to us, it occurred to me that maybe "The Sacrifice of

Isaac" wasn't the worst story for the church fathers to have picked to honor my grandfather. Maybe in some mysterious way Papa's journey into the unseen realm opened his eyes to new insights—non-earthly insights. Maybe "The Sacrifice of Isaac" was the one Bible story that transcends human understanding and maybe this stained glass window was Papa's sign to us that now he understood it.

Unremembered Acts

The best portion of a good man's life is his little,
nameless, unremembered acts of kindness and love.

William Wordsworth

three little turtles
lived with my mother
when she was eight

she can't remember
their names but
she kept them in a bowl

on the window sill
in her room
her father watched

over them one summer
when she and her mother
brothers went to Birmingham

to visit grandparents
her father stayed
behind and fed

the turtles and the dog
every morning and every night
he wrote her letters

about their progress
I found those letters in a box
after my grandmother died

she had carefully ribboned
them for safekeeping
the ones Papa carefully penned

so my mother
could read his words
large bubble letters

printed in black ink
on hot summer's evenings
after a hard day's work

my mother's father
alone in his big house
his children and wife

down in Alabama and he
writing letters about turtles
that my mother can hardly recall

he is gone as are the turtles
and the summers in Alabama
but his yellowed letters

breathe life in my hand
in my heart and the best portion
of this man's life

really does show
after all else
has fallen away

Beau Geste

During the week, my father was usually dressed in suit and tie and wing tip shoes. He worked very hard making a good living as an executive so that my mother and we four siblings could live very comfortably, almost luxuriously, by the 1950s and 1960s standard. On the weekend, however, my father, like Superman, shed his mild mannered businessman's persona and put on the mantle of fantasy. He would dress in comfortable slacks and golf shirt and then sit with us in front of the television, losing himself in the old movies he had so loved in his youth.

We were often transported to the deck of Errol Flynn's pirate ships or to his Sherwood Forest. We had been to Tarzan's tree house and smelled the smoke of the Mummy's sacred tanna leaves. Frankenstein's monster had scared the living daylights out of us, and King Kong gave my sister, Betsy, nightmares for years. We felt "Nearer my God to Thee" as the Titanic slowly sank into icy waters on its maiden voyage, and Shirley Temple tap-danced her way into the hearts of us all. I remember with extreme fondness all those blustery, winter Saturdays and Sundays that we ate Daddy-made popcorn (and sometimes his "infamous" homemade noodle soup) as we watched old movies that he would practically narrate for us.

One of the most touching movie experiences for me was the afternoon that we watched *Beau Geste*. Gary Cooper was the hero and, as I recall, very much like the man I saw and still see my father as—tall and slim and ever the gentleman. The story goes that three boys grow up playing Viking war games together, and they vow that when they become men, they will seek out adventures of a similar sort. They keep their promise because they end up in the French Foreign Legion avoiding arrest for the theft of some jewel. When the fort is under attack and desert warriors hopelessly outnumber the troops, Beau (Gary Cooper) props up fallen comrades at the ramparts to fool the attackers into thinking that there were more Legionnaires than there actually were. When Beau's best friend is killed, Beau gives him a Viking's funeral by burning down the fort with the slain friend ceremoniously laid out, the body of the "dog-of-a-commander" at his feet.

All of us had tears in our eyes, even my father who rarely allowed such unmanly displays of sentiment. Only as an adult have I realized the incredible value of these memories—of my father's sharing a very special part of himself with his children—his dream world. Sharing these precious stories of his youth was indeed making a "beau geste" or "gallant gesture" all his own. As I sit in the darkened movie houses with my own children watching the films of my generation and their generation, I can only hope that they will come to know the value of stories and remember these "movie moments" as fondly as the ones my father shared with us.

Duchess

waits by the gates
of Dad's cold winter
memories—pink-tongued
and golden, a dog fit to lie
at the feet of dead Vikings.
She waits in sunshine,
in snow, for my father
then fourteen,
for my father now old.
Duchess is loyal
unlike my grandfather
who leaves his family, his son,
to sell his wares
to farmers and daughters
in Iowa cornfields.
Duchess stays close
even when Grandmother
withdraws in silence
behind cold winter eyes.
My father's old eyes glisten
at the part when Duchess dies.
He sees himself
cut frozen black ground
with an old rusted ax.
He feels the soft
blanket with Duchess inside.
He watches the young boy,
man, lower her down
again in snowy field memory.
My father still grieves
for Duchess, a dog fit for Vikings,
sixty years dead.

Hardy's Imprint

After thirty-four years of marriage, one could say that the romance should have gone out of my marriage; but it hasn't. There isn't a day that goes by when I am not reminded of why it is I married the man I did. I am terribly grateful for being "lucky in love."

Hardy is a salt-of-the-earth kind of guy who is presently the General Director for Technology in the Duval County School System. In his long career, he has been a principal, a vice principal, an assistant principal and an English teacher, and it is obvious to all who know him that Hardy has been dedicated all his adult life to the education and betterment of our city's youth. I consider him a pillar of the community, but along with that, I consider him a lot of fun. He tells wonderful stories and hysterical jokes; and at parties, people seem to congregate around him. I guess that being around children all the time has kept him young and playful, and I can't get enough of the guy.

I'll never forget when we were much younger. We only had one child at the time and both of us were teaching. Hardy was also coaching the junior varsity football team at Wolfson Senior High School. He was so proud of his winning team and his efforts. After all, he was an English major who had to take on the coaching responsibilities if he was to get a teaching position. The joke was, between the veteran coaches, that the first thing Hardy wanted to know was if the O's and X's on the play diagrams were capitalized or lower case letters.

At any rate, he did very well that year with his players. They won every game that season and were about to play in the junior varsity playoffs. I, the dutiful coach's wife, sat in the bleachers and cheered until I was hoarse. I don't remember the score or any of the plays. All I can remember is that we won, and what happened after the game was over.

I have it all in my head like the scene from a movie. I am on one end of the field and Hardy is at the other. Then in slow motion we approach each other as the crescendo music plays in the background. Closer and closer we get until we are just about in each other's arms. Hardy opens his mouth to smile at me and I stop, dead in my tracks.

Hardy had been chewing tobacco all during the game and his teeth were brown and disgusting. Unaware of how he looked he grabbed me and said, "Hey Babe, how's 'bout a kiss?"

"Eeeewww!" I screamed, averting my face from the kiss I was sure would follow.

We still laugh about that and countless other mishaps of our lives together. I remember the unbuilding of the bicycle to repair it and the unbuilding of the second bike to see how to fix the first. As it turned out, we had to take two boxes of bike parts back to the shop. There is the amazing Hardy-made collapsible step for the camper, and there was the Hardy-made boat trailer that gouged his thigh and required a trip to the emergency room for stitches. I am surprised that the hospital hasn't dedicated a wing to us in honor of all the trips we've made there.

One day when we lived in our small, starter home, I was washing dishes and Hardy was outside mowing the lawn. He was at a stopping place when he came up to the kitchen window and peered in at me. Then with a look of considerable passion, he kissed one of the panes of glass, making a very funny face in the process. I laughed and laughed. He then turned and went about the rest of the yard work. As I gazed out the window after him, I realized that he had left a kiss print on the glass, and seeing it touched my heart very tenderly. This print was representative of the imprint that Hardy has made on my life—funny, gentle and very visible. As far as I know, that kiss print is still there on that one pane of glass, because I never washed it off as long as we lived there. I like to imagine that the new owners of our old house have forgotten to wash it off as well; that the kiss print is still there proudly demonstrating the affection with which I have been generously blessed.

Living with a Man

means having to sleep
without covers
when you want them
windows open

when you want them
closed and tight
means confusion
in the living room

newspaper   glasses
hats and dishes he
forgets to put up
and underwear lost

under the bed so
you don't find them
when they've got
to be ready to wear

for luck in games men play
and you don't understand
or even want to watch
on TV or hear on radio

but this man brings
a joy to your soul
makes you laugh
out loud at antics

and jokes and tickling
and he gets you
not to take the world
so seriously   then when

the cold wind howls
he lets you crawl up
next to his warmth
and stay comforted

facing together the world
which looms too big
for anybody
to face alone

Man's Body Found
AP — Cumberland Island

campers find bony man
sitting   leaning   dead
against a water oak
dressed

in red flannel shirt
in hiking pants and boots
he waits in awe
mouth open

eyes wide   hollow
kudzu vines have kept him
secret from strangers
but raccoons knew just

where to pick his pockets
crows sized him up
for weeks their shadows
touched his upturned face

worn nearly to bone
reporters and police puzzle
he wasn't shot
or mauled by wild boar

he hadn't struggled
under thick oak branches
his wealthy wallet tells them
he was seventy six

that he could drive
and his mother named him
Harold
they covered him

gently with a musty tarp
his shedding fingers
stretching out from under
toward his tooth-worn pipe

no longer warm

Wonderment

Wonderment

During those wonderful, scary years when I was able to stay home as a housewife and mother when our children were little, I experienced many moments of wonder. One such moment came during a special summer when Mandy, my daughter, was all of four years old and Casey, my son, was barely a year. Mandy, who was still not used to this "brother thing," tested my patience on a daily basis. She was constantly vying for my attention, so much so that I had a difficult time even nursing the baby. She would whine to get in my lap or crawl on my shoulders. She would give me no peace, so at the suggestion of a child psychologist I consulted, we invented "together time," a thirty-minute period when Mandy got my undivided and complete attention.

She was very much into the Peter Pan story at the time. Not only did I have to read and reread the story to her every night, but also many a morning I found myself crawling around through the maze of bushes being a crocodile to Mandy's Peter or Wendy. It was worth it, this time together. My daughter seemed to appreciate this attention, and she began to give me some space. I could say to her, "Mandy,

I'll play with you during 'together time', which is in a little while. Now, let me feed the baby." And she would cheerfully say, "Okay," then go her merry way.

Mandy was quite an inventive child. Her fantasies were extremely elaborate and she was just so cute, that I couldn't help but be drawn into her little worlds. She had decided to be Tinkerbell and begged me to help her get some wings. I racked my brain for a few days until I came up with the perfect solution. Using poster board, I made a large pair of fairy wings which Mandy and I colored with crayons. We then devised a complex system of string webbing to secure the wings to her little body. She wore a long yellow party dress, a yellow and green Easter bonnet she had made that spring, a pair of pink plastic little-girl high heels. Then with a magic wand that her grandmother had given her at Halloween the year before, Mandy was transformed into a real, live nymph.

For the rest of that day, she was lost in her fantasy, long after our "together time" was over. It was all I could do to get her to take the wings off so that she could be bathed and put to bed. Her little wings and fairy paraphernalia were carefully laid out in her rocking chair for the next morning's play.

The next day, I awoke and went through the usual morning ritual—coffee, paper and getting my husband off to school. Since school started so early, we adults were up before the children—or so we thought.

At about seven a.m. that day, I received a phone call, which always gets my heart pounding when it comes so early—it seems that only bad news comes like that. At any rate, it was Dorie, one of my neighbors.

"Hey, you lose anything?"

"What are you talking about?" I asked.

"Maybe I should say, 'Have you lost anybody?'"

"Dorie, you're going to have to stop talking in riddles. I haven't the vaguest notion what you are talking about."

"Well," she said, laughing, "I received a small knock on my door this morning and when I opened the door, what do I see but a little, blonde fairy complete with wings and wand wanting to know if I can come out and play."

"Oh, my God!" I gasped. "I'm on my way over."

"Don't rush," Dorie laughed. "We're having a great time. I just thought you'd be relieved to know where your Tinkerbell was."

I hurried out the door and down the street and there, as the sunrays were just breaking through the treetops of the neighborhood, was my fairy princess flitting about on the driveway of my neighbor—wings flopping awkwardly, shoes clicking quickly and arms and wand curving through the air in magical gestures. It was a priceless sight.

Little Girl Memory

little girls sleep little
when they spend the night
giggling
on the sleeping porch

Papa rumbles far away
in darkness
and little girls imagine
a bear

and squeal some more
for hours little girls stab
at shadows
with flashlights

but blue hazy moonlight
still dusts the furniture
with loneliness
little girls grow quiet

when truck tires whine
on highways leading
far away   silent
when train whistles call

and it is then they know
that all things must end
that spending the night
will be over at dawn

that life will be over
too soon   too soon
so little girls sleep
in each others arms

dreaming that no one
will ever let them go

Rainy Days and Mandy

I believe I have always been a supportive and helpful mother, even if I have fallen short of perfection many, many times. I know I tried my best especially when my children were learning the wonders of the free enterprise system. One of Mandy's first jobs was as a concessionaire at the Baymeadows Eight Cinema about three miles from our house. Since she did not have her own car and she was still an underage driver, I had the good fortune of being her driver/chauffeur on the days she worked.

I remember fondly an incident one night as I waited for her to finish the last of her clean-up procedures. It was a hot August or September evening and the weather had been threatening all day long. Clouds had banked as the sun set, and I recall how lovely the sky had been at that time. I had erroneously predicted a calm evening based on the red hue of the evening sky, and admonished myself as large heavy drops of rain began to splatter on my windshield while I waited for my daughter. The drops were sparse at first and dramatically disintegrated before my eyes. Then they were too numerous to count and I was suddenly swallowed in an incredible deluge.

I was really quite cozy in my little Subaru, the torrents pounding the roof in a nearly deafening roar. The streetlights outside caught beautifully the swirls and the sheets of rain in its amber-colored light. It almost looked like snow, but the barely slackening heat was still oppressive so I knew I wasn't in a blizzard.

I cracked the window so the clean smell of the rain could envelope me, and also so that I would not steam up my windows. Then I closed my eyes and listened to the soothing drone pounding on my car roof. I was carried back to the many earlier Florida summers where I would sit as a kid at the picnic table on our screened porch or out in the rockers on our front porch and listen to the daily rainstorms while I let my mind coast. The big elephant ears that grew up against my childhood house loudly caught the roof run-off. The pines swayed gently in the breeze and I could rest from my troubles, because the predictable rains always came and soothed my troubled mind. The million life-giving drops gently touched my life, and I treasure these rainy moments when I am safe and dry, still in the center of a storm. It was like that the night I waited for Mandy. I knew that the rain was refreshing the earth and cleansing the air, and I was beginning to feel a sense of renewal in myself.

I remember one special day when Mandy had discovered the joys of rain and umbrellas. She had been given a red parasol for her fourth birthday and with it were a tiny pair of red galoshes. Mandy insisted upon wearing these three things all day, long before the rains came—even though I had explained all about bad luck if you open an umbrella in the house and all. She became a Gene Kelly, singing-in-the-rain character, only her little-girl songs were sung in the sun—that is, until the afternoon came and with it the threatening storms. Of course, I wouldn't let her out in the worst of the storm, not until all the lightning had subsided and all that remained were errant sprinkles and many luscious mudpuddles. Mandy delighted my mother's heart as she skipped and hopped in her flompy shoes through every puddle in sight—parasol held high and voice carrying on the clean air. Morton Salt would have been proud.

There are other rain memories that I hold dear. I especially love the monster storms that are frequent in Florida. They often occur around the dinner hour and they are frightening and exciting all at the same time. Giant, gray to black clouds form at some point of the compass, usually the west, although not always. The contrast is striking between the storm and the fair weather it seems to be pursuing. Then, as in my nightmares, the rolling dark clouds take on the shape of tidal waves threatening to swallow me alive. My heart beats faster. My cats start returning home from their journeys or prowls and seek shelter under my bed. The pine trees are whipped about, as are my maples, and the magnolia tree deposits a layer of scurrying leaves upon the lawn. Thunder begins to roll and then in a climactic moment, the sky opens up and pours. Occasionally we lose power, then we get out the candles and enjoy the storm with only the rain and thunder filling our ears, soothing our "uppity" and appliance-dependent sensibilities.

The rain had slowed somewhat when a panting and very damp Mandy quickly opened the car door, startled me out of my daydream, and flopped into the seat next to me. She still smelled of popcorn.

"Done!" she said, as if punctuating the memories for me. The storm was indeed drawing to a close. I started up the car, and we drove carefully through the diminishing sprinkles back to drier realities and home.

Fireflies at Fort Clinch

At first we thought that our campfire had spewed sparks through the air behind us, because we had built a pretty big fire from a large pile of pine logs; but it wasn't that at all. The sparkly cloud that appeared in the nearby encampment looked like phosphorescent bubbles emerging from black, night waves.

"What do you suppose that is?" my husband and I asked each other, our eyes squinting, trying to make out exactly what the ghostlike cloud was. After a few seconds of intense scrutiny, I realized that there was something amazingly familiar about this shape. It was a swarm of fireflies with tiny, pale green flashes that sparkled in the night like emeralds in a deep, dark mine.

I was instantly transported back to a distant time. As a child I could often be found out on the summer lawn dressed in short sleeves and shorts, running around in the half dark, trying to catch the elusive specks of light in my hands as if to save their energy. Only once did I ever catch any and put them in a jar, a mayonnaise jar that Mama provided me to use as firefly zoos. The disastrous results of dead insects in the morning convinced me to catch fireflies only for a brief moment and then only in the cupped palms of my hands where I could peek in and observe their flashing miracle. Then I would have to let them go to lighten someone else's night.

Fireflies were and still remain a magnificent mystery. It is said that even scientists cannot figure how it is they can generate light without generating heat, but to a child such things are not important. What is important to a child is that fireflies come in the summer and fill the air with magic. Blink on here. Blink off. Blink on in a new place. Blink off. Blink on far away.

And so it was with the camping trip of April 1991, when my husband and I took the kids to Fort Clinch State Park at Fernandina Beach, Florida. Fireflies were swarming near us in numbers I had not thought possible, and my children were awakened to the magic just as I had been all those long summers ago. They jumped up once they realized what the specks were and swooped over to catch in their little hands all the magic they could hold. Add to this the silvery reflections of the nearly full moon on the slippery oak leaves and the little nymph-like bodies of two children. Then the forest we camped in became a fairy world.

My husband and I wandered over to watch our little pixies dance with the fireflies. They weren't able to catch any, of course, being unused to the rigors of firefly entrapment because civilization had driven these insects further and further out of town. Still, my son and daughter squealed with the same delight I had known as a child chasing fireflies.

Later, after all the cavorting was finished and the tiny sparkles had dissolved into the thin air, our exhausted children fell into our arms from all their dancing. The drone of ship engines out in the St. Mary's River was all that was civilized in our world.

Blueberry Morning

One of my favorite children's books was one I have read at least a dozen times to my children. *Blueberries for Sal,* a charming story by Robert McClosky, was about the morning Sal and her mother went blueberry picking in Vermont, I believe. While doing so, they encounter a bear and her cub.

Maybe it was this book that got me inspired, but soon after I had first read it to my children, I was scouring the classified ads to find blueberry fields or groves (or whatever you call them) that were ready for "you-pick" customers. Since then, my children and I have been to the Northside, the Westside and the Southside and picked the finest blueberries this side of Eden.

The routine was this. We would awaken before the sun was up on a warm morning in the latter part of May or early June. After a little breakfast and dressing appropriately, we would pile into the car with the classified ad circled in red and directions to get there scribbled in the margins. Then, as the sun came up and my children came to full consciousness, we would find these lovely mist-filled places with rows of blueberry bushes and lots and lots of blueberries.

With sandcastle pails in our hands and tremendous desire in our hearts, we set off down the rows collecting the sweet, blue treasure. Excited little hands carefully plucked the ripe fruit and deposited it in the pails; but sometimes these hands missed their mark and the fruit would be accidentally deposited in the mouth.

We would continue in this pattern for at least two hours, which is a very long time for small children; but my two tow-headed bundles of energy were inspired and looking for the bears to come, I imagine. All we ever saw of a dangerous nature were bees. One grove had a hive dead center of the bushes.

"Helps with the pollination process," the farmer told us. "Bees won't hurt you none if you don't swat at 'em."

The bees didn't hurt us either. They buzzed around us busily, and never in all our journeys did one so much as land on us.

Every year that we picked blueberries, our goal was to get ten or more pounds. When we thought we were getting close to that end, we would deposit our booty in the scales and paid the farmer his asking price. We then carried home a year's worth of summer in Zip-Lock™ bags.

All berries were taken home to freeze, except for the one cupful needed to make an immediate batch of blueberry muffins. Soon the kitchen smelled of baked goods and good times that mothers keep close and children will fondly remember when they have their own children and summer mornings together.

Now, whenever I go to the grocery and I find myself drawn to the plastic cartons of very expensive berries, I remember the wonderful blueberry experiences I have had. If I still have any berries left in the freezer, I just pass the grocery berries by. If I don't, I go ahead and buy a small basketful just to remind me of how wonderful life can be— even when it is winter and blueberry days are far in the future.

Blueberries

busy stained fingers
touch the ripe fruit
snap each from moorings
then drop it to heaps
of picked berries

collected in yellow buckets
we once used for sand castles
my little ones and I
gather berries
on a morning worth remembering

their towheads bob
two rows away from me
my head bobs slower
I am methodical and gleaning
each branch of its harvest

my children are so quick
they cannot wait to hurry away
they miss the best fruit
and I cannot stop them
or this morning

the early sun is slow
and oozing down pine trees
like thick flowing honey
we must shade our eyes
from its richness

the jays watch our progress
scolding our presence
that steals all their bounty
our buckets grow heavy
my children grow tired

the day has warmed us
so we get back into car seats
and drive home to muffins
we pack with blue treasure
and drink with cool milk

Bus Rides and Little Kids

Back in a distant time of my marriage, when the children were little and I had the privilege of staying home from my job to be with them, I recall that the children and I had to find inexpensive ways to entertain ourselves. Our pleasures were not as austere as the pitiful pleasures my grandmother would tell of the Depression—only getting an orange for Christmas and maybe a walnut. Like the Joad family in The *Grapes of Wrath*, my husband and I had a car, but it had to be used to transport him on his job. The children and I had to find inventive ways to get around while he was at work. We were within walking distance of the grocery store and the pediatrician, so we had our survival needs met. It was just that getting to extravagant places like movies or malls proved difficult and challenging.

Fortunately, we were within two blocks of a bus stop where a bus could carry us to the heart of the big city, Jacksonville. It was our greatest adventure to scrounge up the $1.50 change for the round trip to Hemming Park and take a day trip to May Cohens Department Store in the St. James Building downtown. Early in the morning of any week day, we might bundle up or dress down as the weather dictated and climb aboard an air conditioned bus to be jostled gently all the way to whatever lay ahead.

I can see Mandy, my little five-year-old princess, on her knees looking out the window, fogging the glass in the process as she took in every morsel of sensation. Everything was magic to her as the ponderous bus lumbered through neighborhoods, picking up passengers.

"Look Mama! Look!" she'd tell me in a joyful voice. Casey my two year old was fascinated more by all the hardware the bus had to offer—he loved the buzzers and straps and wheel wells and screws. It was all I could do to get him to keep from dismantling the seat.

As we came nearer the town, we could see the great drawbridges that cross the St. Johns River. I can remember that when I first moved to Florida, these bridges were as architecturally amazing to my family as the pyramids at Giza would have been. Imagine that a bridge could move up and down and allow boats to pass under it all while the rush hour traffic above was brought to a standstill! Imagine the power the bridge had to bring the city to a complete halt! My father always got out of his car and watched the process—Yankee that he was—and for years I thought that only in Florida did these bridges exist.

Every bus journey required that we cross the great blue bridge—the Main Street Bridge— and every time that we did so, the children stopped in their activities and were held silently spellbound by the sound of the tires on the grate and the "Whoosh! Whoosh! Whoosh!" of the blue girders that arched overheard as we passed by.

We disembarked at the park near the department store and with fast but little tiny baby steps, we hurried to May Cohens. We entered through tricky, but fascinating revolving doors and were quickly enveloped by the enormity of the building. Three stories high with a mezzanine and a basement! And escalators too! What a wonderland! During the Christmas season, we had to hurry to Santa Land on the third floor to see the jolly, old elf himself. Then we'd go from floor to floor "window shopping" on the inside and imagining what we'd buy if we could only win the lottery. During the summer, we wandered the bargain basement displays in the hopes that cheap treasure could be discovered. Sometimes we were lucky. Most of the time we were not.

No matter what the season, we always gravitated toward the candy counter located in the very heart of the store on the ground floor. Here, the many compartments of creamy of chocolates and fudges made even my mouth water. The colorful sugar coated jellies and jelly beans made the children dance and jump in anticipation as the sales clerk handed me the white paper bag filled with 50 cents worth of these delights all just the right size for little kids to nibble.

The most difficult part of our journey was when I might want to try on clothes. Neither of the children really wanted to cooperate with this procedure. Mandy would quite frequently whine, "Let's go, Mama," as I'd drag the two reluctant children into the dressing room. I'd put her off by saying it would just be a few more minutes and then we'd have some more fun.

The children soon discovered that the clothes racks could be a forest through which they would run and hide. Casey became very adept at this. Twice I recall the panic I felt when I couldn't see him and thought he was lost. Actually he was but a few feet away in a rack of pleated, wool skirts, and call as I might, he thought it great sport to be quiet. My mother's fearful heart pounded painfully at the thought of losing my baby, and just about that time I was ready to call out the house police, he'd emerge all smiles and giggles. I soon realized that it was time to move on.

As a final treat, we would have lunch in Cohen's own restaurant. The children would usually order hot dogs or hamburgers and I would eat what they didn't want. Sometimes we got to have an ice cream, especially if we had been good little boys and girls, and we always were. It was just so neat to be eating in a grown-up place with all the executives from the businesses across the streets crowding the tables. We really didn't fit in, but we always felt welcomed.

When we had finally exhausted ourselves, it was time to make the trip home. We sat quietly on a bench in the park and waited for our bus to return. When it finally arrived, we'd get on, take our seats, and all but me would fall into an exhausted sleep. It was always a big day. It was always a sweet memory. And every time a big, old bus lumbers past me as I go about my business in a car all my own, I think of those lovely times when pleasures were simple and everywhere were things at which to marvel.

Express Bus

one little girl
one mama
with a handhold too tight
and feet that were swollen
boarded the 4:55
took their silent places
waited for rocking motions
to carry them
all the way home

afternoon light
sliced through alleys
department store shadows
bus windows

the little girl glistened
in reflections
her tired mother
faded in darkness
burdened
by too many tradeoffs

Look Mama
I'm pretty

Don't be prideful
an exhausted voice
finding a mark

Casey Beach Day

It lives in my heart as one of the happiest times I've ever lived. To be sure it wasn't as joyous as those moments when I heard for the first time the crying of my newborn infants or the moment when my husband-to-be said that he loved me for the first time. It was, however, way up there on the happiness scale—that day Casey and I went to the beach all by ourselves.

We had just deposited Mandy at the Presbyterian Day School. She was four and driving me crazy thinking up things for her to do. The school was her fun haven, and it provided me with a short respite wherein I could renew myself for a few hours, at least. On that October morning, it occurred to me that I wanted to be near the sea. So I loaded my toddler son, Casey, into his car seat and we headed east. Twenty minutes hadn't passed before we found ourselves at Jacksonville Beach at the edge of the Atlantic Ocean. We stopped at a Seven/Eleven™ and bought a package of powdered doughnuts, a cup of hot coffee for me and a bottle of apple juice for Casey. We then proceeded to and parked at the nearest public access to the beach. With a blanket and son on one arm and our "picnic" bag in the other, I trudged through about fifty yards of sand to settle on a blanket for the morning.

There weren't five people on the beach that morning, even counting ourselves. The sun was low in the autumn sky, but it was golden and already warm. The tide was low and the murmur of the blue-green waves sounded soothing and soft.

I can still see Casey running for the water—all twenty or twenty-one pounds of him giggling and squealing as he chased flocks of seagulls that flurried up into the sky like a smoky cloud. His golden ringlets of hair tousled in the unusually warm breeze and his chubby baby legs were almost a blur as he ran. It was glorious. He was a tremendous bundle of energy and delight. Back and forth he went—down to the waves and back up to me, his tiny teeth flashing in his bright smiles.

I was able to coax him to stay on the blanket with me briefly while we enjoyed our doughnuts, coffee and juice. He had barely finished one doughnut when he was back up on his feet and running. As he looked back at me over his shoulder as he left me, I caught a glimpse of his beautiful, sugary face. It was a perfect moment.

For the two and a half hours we spent there, Casey never stopped. He brought me a treasure trove of sea shells, including a dead crab. He waded through and eventually swam in a tiny slough that had formed near us. He ate every last doughnut and crumb he could find. Of course, he probably got as much sand in his mouth as he did sugar, but he didn't seemed bothered by it and I figured it would all pass sooner or later.

As the appointed leaving hour approached, I dreaded having to remove my son from the paradise we had found for ourselves. I was afraid that he'd cry and carry on, but he didn't. As I scooped him up—soggy play suit and all—into my arms to carry him back to the car, he just put his little boy arms around my neck and held on tight. I dressed him in dry diaper and fresh shirt, and he slept all the way back to the city.

Casey's Touch

I die in dreams
that wake my son
and send him
trembling
to my bed

he clings
to my neck
his nightmare voice
whispering sadness

he watched me
a smiling mother
ghost drifting toward him
his outstretched hand
passed through my cheek
his hug squeezed
through my waist

I disappeared

in the darkness
I tell him
I'm still here

with substantial arms
I cling to him
my little boy facing
the future of mothers
the future of sons

we are losing each other
as we grow up

his touch
even now
feels faint

New Beginnings and The Empty Nest

I don't know what it is about painting, but I seem to feel a need to cover the walls of my life as I pass through each phase of existence. I painted the walls of my room when I became a teenager. When I got married and moved into my first home, I got out the paint cans and roller. When my husband and I first found out we were going to have a baby, I was suddenly drawn to the local paint store for nursery hues; and now it has happened again. Suddenly I felt the urge to slather a layer of fresh paint all over the walls and ceilings of my house this summer—the summer of my empty nest.

My son Casey, the second and last of my children, will be out the door and off to college in a few days, and as joyous as that may be on the surface, I fear the great hole his absence will create in the lives of my husband and myself. Oh, I know in my head that this is all part of the grand scheme of life and that I should be dancing in the streets. I will have a reduction of laundry to do, fewer dishes to clean, and there will always be cookies in the jar when I want one. Still, I can't help but get choked up when I find in the medicine cabinet several baby teeth left years ago by the Tooth Fairy, as I prep the bathroom for painting.

I have to fight tears as I find photographs of my son in his Yoda Halloween costume under the dresser I had moved so I could get the paint to the wall. And I can't help but wonder how I'll handle all the cleanliness as I scrape off the spaghetti noodle my son threw against the kitchen wall to see if his dinner was ready.

Mothers have been dealing with this "departure painting" since the advent of the paint can, I suppose. My own mother, who had to send off four children, hired professionals to come and redecorate the whole house when the last of us left. When I beheld my old home for the first time, I took a sharp breath. It was beautiful, but it looked more like a magazine display than my home. Maybe that was the point. If it seemed too familiar to the "fledglings," then maybe they would find their way back to the "nest" and never want to leave.

I don't think disguising the place so the kids couldn't recognize it was what motivated me to paint this year. I just think that I need a "clean slate" every so often in my life. This new, childless phase of my life needed to be marked in some manner, and my past behavior should have been a clue to me as I shelled out major bucks for the Power Painter™. As in all phases of my life, I wanted a "fresh start." For the same reasons that I make New Year's resolutions and birthday wishes; for the same reason that I wanted a new notebook each school year and new clothes for new jobs; I wanted a new space in which to conduct my new life—a life without all those scraped-kneed, bony little boys bouncing on my sofa; a life without jelly-jar weed bouquets and bug specimens all over the house. I needed to spiff up my surroundings for whatever adventures lay ahead of me.

The hardest part of this summer's paint job was encountering the door jamb of my bedroom where we had penciled in the growth progress of each of my children. On April 5, 1990, my son was just over four feet tall and by September of 1994, the last time we actually measured, he had grown over a foot and a half. Now he towers over me, and I marvel as I remember holding his little squirming body on my shoulder when he cried as an infant so long ago; so very recently in my heart. I couldn't paint over the marks, even as unsightly as it might be to the sensibilities of those who have a higher standard of tidiness than I. I just painted around the precious marks and dates, leaving that job for some future owner of this house.

And now that everything is pristine and perfect—now that the drapes have been cleaned, the carpets have been shampooed and the windows have been washed—I am ready. It's just that I'm not really sure for what.

Seeing a Great Light

I learned to walk
in darkness when my baby
cried at night
through moonless rooms

negotiating bedposts—chairs
I roughed the surface
of soft hair
with sightless fingers

felt the squirming
contour of a little body
wild with fear
I became darkness

a black warm shadow
taking tiny sobs
in shadow arms
and singing very gently

not to cry
not to cry

my baby's gone now
she walks through
her own darkness
to find her tiny warmth

but I still wander
through my night
sometimes looking
with my fingers

hands   becoming
all warm and dark again
the cradle is empty
but I am filled full

of memories   peace
and I need no sleep
just soft gentle darkness
to hold me

Treasure

Treasure

Every family has its treasure—a grandmother's silver tea service, an aunt's imported china, an anniversary necklace or a variety of rings; but not all the treasures of a family have a good, fair market value. Some of the treasures are valuable only because the owner has some special connection to the treasure that takes it beyond price.

There are three such treasures in my family. One is a Rose of Sharon quilt my great-grandmother made for my mother's wedding day. Another is a great, black iron skillet that my grandfather made for my mother, also a wedding present. The last is a baby's music box that plays Brahms' Lullaby. All of these things have tremendous value to me. They would not cost a great deal in the open market, but what they represent to me about family is priceless.

Each time I look at the quilt my great-grandmother made, not only can I see in my mind the innumerable sacks of flour—sacks that gave up their cheerful, floral skins to become a work of art—but I can also see her thimbled, skilled hands working late into the evenings after a hard day of baking, scrubbing and canning. I can make out the remnants of many familiar dresses and shirts that became a part of this masterpiece, which would keep little girls warm on blustery nights or would serve as a tent for little girl games on rainy days.

I never met my great-grandmother. She died before I was born, so I can only guess at her personality; but if the work of her hand is any indication of the person who made it, she was indeed an intricate, strong woman who knew the value of hard work and industry. I can see it in the carefully wrought designs of fabric. I can feel it in the near seamless stitchery.

My grandfather, in a foundry in Birmingham, Alabama, where he was a foreman, forged the big, black skillet. He was a large, imposing man, who in his day had drop-dead good looks. To my way of thinking, there was nothing that my grandfather couldn't do. I can just imagine his tremendous, gloved hands turning the ladles to pour the molten iron into the appropriate skillet mold. These hands that could lift such heavy things could also tie ribbons in my little-girl hair. Each Sunday these hands could be seen folded in prayer at the Methodist church at the foot of the hill where he lived.

Thanks to his labor, his gift to my mother provided countless fried chicken dinners for my family and me when I was a child. I cannot see his skillet that my mouth doesn't begin to water, and I long for those lazy, Sunday dinners served right after church. Although we have more efficient cookware now, we would never part with the old black monster.

The baby's music box is the least imposing of our treasures. It is made of plastic and is as plain and unexciting as unflavored yogurt. I can't even remember how I acquired the little box. It used to sit on the dresser in the nursery of my children, and I used to crank it up every time I had diapers to change or babies to rock.

One day recently, I discovered it as I was doing some major spring-cleaning. It was in some nondescript box in a closet, and my accidental jousting of it activated the little song. Tears filled my eyes as I remembered all those special and often difficult nights with my little ones. As the diminutive box whirred and spun out its music, I remembered little dresses and tiny pants and toy trucks and bedtime stories. And it was all wonderful memory.

My grandfather and his mother have been dust now for a very long time, and my children have long since moved out of the nursery and into their busy lives. The treasures I associate with these people, however, are better than gold. Every time I spread that glorious quilt upon the bed, my great-grandmother is alive. Every time I unearth the old black skillet from under the aluminum pots, my grandfather lives, and every time I hear the music box play, my children are little and safe in their beds again. It is then that I know what is truly important. It is then that I know what real value is, and it has little to do with money.

Quilting Harvest

sunning on clothes lines
at the antique store
ten or twelve quilts
breathe on the breeze

hum with stories
told at bees where
busy fingers
thimbled/strong

knew the passage
of each tiny stitch
knew the patterns
how they fell

in the gathering darkness
of afternoon storms
proprietors rush
to gather in arms

all the scraps of ties
party dresses
Sunday go to
meeting clothes

collected in the rows
of patchwork design
then pile them warm
in stacks like harvest hay

Grandmother's Window

I can remember being four or five years old and standing before the massive picture window at my grandmother's house as the morning sun streamed in. The sill began where my chin ended, and I often rested my head and elbows on it so I could gaze long moments at the multitude of colors created by the array of knick-knacks set out on the shelves Papa, my grandfather, had erected there. Red carnival glass goblets cast their fiery passion across the room. Blue Venetian glass slippers dazzled like Cinderella shoes. Topaz yellow blown-glass canaries perched quietly near pale green glass saltcellars. Baby blue cut-glass match holders caught the sunlight like prisms and cast little rainbows all about the room when the sun came in at the right angle. All the while the creeping vines of houseplants wove their way about the twinkling treasures that mesmerized my young eyes.

Breakfast was always a cheery time at my maternal grandparents' Texas house. Not only because we children were on vacation, but also because there were fresh-picked blackberries to put on the cereal during those summer months when we came to visit. Here we would break our fast in a dining room with the marvelous window that sparkled like a carnival at night. Here we would laugh out loud with Papa over the funnies from the newspaper that he would read to us. Here we would bask in the love that Grandmama demonstrated with lavish hugs and praise, as lavish as the rich colors of her wonderful window.

No chest of treasure could have been more precious than these pieces of glass my grandmother had collected throughout her life and displayed in the window of my childhood memory. And when the sorrowful time came for my widowed grandmother to sell her home and move to a nursing home, when she asked for us grandchildren to go through her earthly possessions and take what we wanted, these beautiful knickknacks were the only things of hers I wanted to keep.

The carnival glass candleholder rests in my morning windowsill which occasionally catches the light, but never as spectacularly as the window in my grandmother's house. The yellow canary perches on a shelf in my yellow bathroom, chirping a silent song in the shower's humidity. The blue Venetian glass slipper stands on my mantle and the light blue glass match holder sits on my desk, holding an array of local fossils my children have found. The saltcellars sit on my counter top near my spice rack.

I don't know what it is that makes me cling to these old things. I find that the older I get the more important childhood memories become. I guess that is why so many people hang on to their "junque." Each item has importance in some distant time and place, and it is that place we return to when the going gets rough. These were the places where we felt safe and burden-free. The red color of a grandmother's goblet reminds us of simpler times. Seeing her Cinderella glass slipper carries us right back to the magic stories that once filled our little ears.

Grandparents live again when we see their glass canaries sparkle like bird songs in our windows, letting summer memories fill our hearts. Suddenly, fresh-picked blackberries are possible again, and we find ourselves floating blissfully back to childhood simplicity—if only for a moment.

Grandfather's Cane

the mountain laurel cane
is all twisted and gnarled
like my grandfather was

when he lay dying
in a bed placed
in our living room

where we all could watch
his pain   his suffering
I was just a little girl

not really understanding
what was going on
so it was only

natural that one day
when they brought him food
and he still slept

I tiptoed to his bed
and tray   watered up
at the sight of peaches

shiny, yellow, juicy
beckoning my tiny hand
to take one small sliver

pop it into my mouth
before the man could see
as I trembled

and reached out
the painful smack
of his laurel wood cane

fell across my little hand
I'm not dead yet
the old man rumbled

I never went back
near him ever again
until now

when a cane
so like his very own
at the garage sale

called me to buy it
to reverence
a painful lesson

and the one who taught it

Pony Prints

Not long ago, as I was taking a walk along St. Augustine Road, the fall sun streaming brilliantly through the trees, I noticed something as I looked down upon the pavement. There were at regular intervals impressions of little hooves. For every square of concrete, there were two tiny and very clearly visible hoof prints, as if a pony had cavorted playfully across the not-nearly-dry cement that some workman had so carefully smoothed and prepared.

I couldn't help but smile, remembering that at one time, this segment of road was indeed very rural, especially when my family and I first moved here in 1958. At that time about all that existed around here (other than a few housing developments) was Skinner's Dairy and about five thousand roaming cows. Where apartments and stores are now, there had been green fields stretching to the edge of blue green, pine forests.

The land where the University Albertson's now stands had been a little farm, and on it—by my count—were two horses and one pony or foal. Every time my family and I would ride past on our way to church or to the Lakewood Pharmacy, I would peer out the window hoping to get a glimpse of those fleet-footed creatures that I would have given my eye teeth to have ridden myself, or better yet, owned. Perhaps these were the very horses that had left their tell-tale mark for me to find impressed in concrete some twenty or thirty years later. Maybe not.

I also remember that, tucked back in the woods near the Lakewood housing development, was a house that had a little shed and two Shetland ponies in it. I recall seeing one of the ponies and a little girl rider as late as 1975. Even as an adult, I envied that child whose youth had in it a pony that could be part of games and playful imaginings. Perhaps she was the "leaver-of-hoof prints." Perhaps on a distant autumn day, that little girl was on a scouting mission to check for Timucuan natives. Maybe she was on a mission to deliver some vital message to settlers on the border of the county. Maybe she was totally unaware that her path was undried concrete and that many years later, I would be able to tell that she and her mount had passed that way.

Not long after I had discovered the hoof prints in the concrete, the city began a sewer up-sizing, which required that all the sidewalks with pony marks be torn up. At first I was heartsick thinking that all evidence of someone's joyful day was to be scraped away in the matter of an afternoon. I even considered asking for one of the concrete pieces, one with very clear markings, to put in my garden so that I could keep alive the memory of the ponies. I soon realized that I would never have been able to lift even the smallest piece of concrete to get it in the trunk of my car, so I had to settle for a piece of memory, which is much more portable and longer lasting.

My hope is that one day in the far distant future, when archaeologists are excavating our civilization, they will come across some tiny, rusty horseshoes left along this stretch of road. They will imagine us to have been a happy people since our children rode ponies on beautiful autumn mornings.

Overgrown

I retraced old paths
quite by accident
discovered an earlier
place of pure joy

where horses waited
for me to ride in ten/one
hour lessons to master
the trot and cantor

and gallop—I rode
the winds after my tenth
birthday on palominos
sixteen hands high

and old and gentle
enough for little
daydreamer girls who longed
for real horses—I found

the old road
as a grown up looking
for another road
my busy life needed

the gateway to childhood
was overgrown with kudzu
weeds tangled the road
the horses were gone

dead or moved on
to greener pastures
but summer morning sun
misted the moment

misted my eyes
with a glorious glow
I was at peace
for having the remembrance

went on my way
renewed and young again

Dandelions

There is no denying that Americans are involved in a multimillion dollar campaign toward the annihilation of weeds—crabgrass, dollar weeds, nut grass and deer grass and, of course, there is the ever popular dandelion; but there can also be no denying that a yard filled with the tiny, yellow blossoms fills me with some kind of unearthly delight.

I came around the corner on a walk one June evening and what should I behold but a vacant house's yard teeming with dandelion blossoms. Happily they bobbed in the evening breeze and caught the sunset's glow quite magically. It took my breath away, the way it would have done me as a child. If I hadn't been in my late forties, I might have run laughing into the midst of the flowers and gathered them up in a childlike bouquet. If I hadn't been busy with thoughts of sinus woes and hay fever bouts, I'd have breathed in the musty odor of the happy pedals and moved into a distant memory place. I'd be dressed in corduroy overalls and running amok through joyous fields finding flowers to take home and place in empty mayonnaise jars that my mother kept stored in a pantry for my bug menageries and hand picked gifts.

Oh, the garlands that could be made from these precious weeds? I have made countless, saffron-colored crowns, necklaces and bracelets to enhance my little girl's appearance. Of course, I was careful not to taste the bitter, milky sap that could coat the fingers, unlike the sweet taste of honeysuckle blossoms we would often purposely taste each June. And sometimes I had to intersperse clover blossoms in between when the dandelion season was drawing to a close.

I was also any number of fairy queens in my imaginary heyday. Once I was Guenievere holding forth over all the court with a wave of my weed-draped hand. Another time I was Pocahontas, flower covered and ready for my "brave" to carry me off into the sunset. My bicycle steed was often strewn with blankets of yellow, a poor imitation of the black-eyed Susan blanket Kentucky Derby winners receive. We rode many miles together.

But the best part was the wishing—remember? When the time was right, the blossoms were spent and turned to fuzzy, gray seed ball. I would snatch the stem up to the lips and blow with heavy breath, all the while wondering where the little germ of life would be carried on the wind—maybe even going as far as little girl dreams could travel.

"Make a wish," I had been told by someone older than I, and I did. I wished with all my heart. I wished for a real pony and a baby sister and all the ice cream I could stand to eat whenever I wanted, even if it meant spoiling my appetite. I wished for other things I can't really remember, but I feel very certain that with the exception of the pony and a baby brother before I got that sister, my wishes have, for the most part, come true.

Of course, the actual reality of that seed journey was the germination of many more weeds in neighbors' yards. I can just imagine the really foul words from homeowners when their pristine lawns would produce scraggily offspring. As a child I had no idea this is what my desire for good fortune could do. Only as a teenager and a biology student did I come to understand.

Even so, I try to remember from "whence cometh the weed" as I pluck unwanted pesky plants from my lawn and spray like the rest of my neighbors. Each handful of weed makes me try to imagine a little girl somewhere, yellow garlands in her hair making a good future for herself. Then I try not to mind.

The Magnolia Tree and Me

Ever since I have moved into my present house ten years ago, I have had this running battle—a love/hate relationship—with an enormous, but beautiful magnolia tree that grows in my backyard. It is true that it is a magnificent tree, towering at least three stories into the sky. And its giant canopy provides shade that is sweet and cool, but this magnificent tree makes me absolutely crazy. It sheds constantly—gigantic, slick, brown leaves that are hard to rake and take forever to decompose.

Not that I am opposed to deciduous trees, mind you. I love maples, which shed their leaves in the fall, and I love live oak trees that lose their leaves in the spring, but they have the courtesy to lose their leaves all at once and are done with it. Not my magnolia tree. I have had to do my very best to love my magnolia, because I am constantly picking up after it. All year round, in the cold and in the heat; in wind and rain—leaves come down in a dizzying array.

There are times when I actually feel like some kind of cosmic joke is being played upon me. No sooner do I have the yard raked than a gust of wind litters my yard with 50 to 100 leaves. No sooner than the lawn mower is tidied away in the shed and I turn to admire my handiwork—than a fistful of envelope-sized leaves are floating gently down to mock me.

I have tried all manner of tricks to keep up with the leaves. Once I tried to compost them, but they apparently have a half-life the same as uranium. I then decided to scoop them into plastic and paper bags, which I would leave lying about in strategic positions. I even tried just picking the leaves up with my bare hands as if they were an air-tossed deck of cards. This system worked very well until my 45 year old back began to complain. Mulching the leaves with the lawn mower seemed to be the answer for a while until the grass began to look choked by the brown residue that was left behind. After that, I began to bag the lawn mower clippings in that heavy contraption on the back. Mowing with the big bag is a heavy and tiring procedure, and one that I most often practice now.

I have tried the nail-on-the-end-of-a-rake-handle trick. This works extremely well except that a nail can only accommodate so many skewered leaves, and this procedure is only good for less than 100 leaves, because more leaves would require as much time as mowing would.

One might wonder why I just don't have the tree cut down and hauled away. I almost did once when my cat, Jones, climbed to the top of the magnolia and then promptly fell to earth with a great thud. The poor cat had to be placed in the "intensive cage unit" at the vets until we were sure he would survive. Later, as I considered removing the tree, it occurred to me that my cat's accident was not the fault of the tree, so the magnolia won a reprieve.

I have to admit that the tree is a magnificent being, though. I am impressed by its size and the peaceful atmosphere that it creates under is branches. Many of my potted plants have found a good home at its feet, and many a summer afternoon I find myself under its protective shelter reading my books. *Jurassic Park* was all the more enjoyable when I could look over at the brontosaurus leg-sized magnolia trunk and get into the spirit of the novel. Here too novels with Florida settings like *Sugar Cage* by Connie May Fowler or *The Yearling* by Marjorie Kinnan Rawlings are all the more real.

I have finally made peace with this tree mostly by surrendering to its nature and letting it do what it must. I try not to be too grouchy when I have to rake again and again, or I have to spear the errant leaves with my homemade skewer. I look at it as my karma to be a leaf-raker forever, just as Sisyphus is an eternal rock roller. Besides, it serves no useful purpose to fight it. As a result, I now sense that the tree may have compromised with me just a little. It seems that there was one whole week in December of 1995 that I recall no leaves falling at all. I took it as a good sign.

The Christmas Cactus

In that January when my mother in-law gave it to me, it was still in its white, plastic pot with $1.39 written in grease pencil on the side. She had rescued from the grocery store the three green and scraggly-looking shoots emanating from a little root ball, she said. Truly, the little cactus was most unspectacular. I put it in my kitchen window, mostly to get it out of my way, and every few days when it began to pucker up, I'd give it a little drink of water.

This inauspicious relationship between my Christmas cactus and me continued for quite sometime—until March or May—when it became obvious that the little creature was root-bound. I moved it to a larger, clay pot that was still small enough to sit on the sill of my kitchen window. This new arrangement seemed to agree with the little plant. It developed new limb sections—first red, then light green—at the tips of its branches, and it got bigger and stronger to where it almost looked good. I gave it a shot of Peter's Special every once in a while, and we co-existed very nicely.

July, August and September passed as I went about my summer kitchen business. The little cactus went about his growing while I placed the ripening tomatoes next to him and allowed the peaches to unharden there also. October came and went as did the strawberry jam I'd put up. Then came Thanksgiving with its sumptuous turkey and pies and laid-back days off. It wasn't until early December that I first noticed a pink formation at the end of each shoot, which got larger as the time sped toward Christmas.

Suddenly, one mid-December morning, I entered my kitchen to see three, spectacular, hot-pink blossoms stretching themselves toward me as if to give me a hug. Great, long, delicate pink petals curled in my direction and I was awed.

I had seen cacti blossoms before, usually on the sly since I kept most cacti outside, and their flowers usually folded up before I could get out there to notice; but this Christmas cactus opened up to me in a way that was almost human, and I fell in love with him at that very moment.

Ten years have passed since that December and the three shoots have multiplied twenty- or thirty-fold. Gradually larger pots replaced the first clay pot, until the cactus could no linger sit on my window sill. Now, he lives in a giant pot under my magnolia tree in the backyard where I can see him as I work in the kitchen.

Each December, just a few days before Christmas, every branch of my cactus holds a glorious explosion of pink. I then move him indoors to a place of honor in the living room—near the Christmas tree. Here guests and relatives "ooh and ah" about this incredible beast of a plant. He has become a part of my family's Christmas celebration.

"When are you going to bring *The Cactus* in?" my daughter always asks.

"May I carry *The Cactus* in for you, Dear?" my husband always offers.

"Hey, Mom, where are you going to put *The Cactus* this year?" my son always wonders.

For me *The Cactus*, like the season, has come to symbolize hope. How in the face of incredible indifference, this little, unseemly plant transformed itself into the life-affirming embodiment of glory–and I, for one, am most joyful that this Christmas cactus came into my life.

The Magic of Trains

Every night that I get to have my bedroom windows open, I can hear the trains in the train yard that is located just a few miles north of my house. The sounds coming from there are actually very comforting and reassuring. The familiar clanging and the booming and the chugging are not too close or loud that they would disturb my sleep. They just carry me back to earlier times in my life when trains were something to behold and get excited about.

When my brother and I were little, we used to get all fired up at the approach of a train. Those cross arms would go down in front of our father's old black Ford, and we could feel the earth trembling as the train approached. Daddy always suggested that we wave at the engineer (now called an engine man—or engine person?), and we'd wave our little arms and hands until we could barely hold them up. As if by magic, those engineers and caboose firemen always waved back. Gleefully we'd squeal and jump as if we had attained a great achievement.

I also remember the wonderful trips my mother, brother, sisters and I would make on the train to Fort Worth, Texas, to visit my maternal grandparents. Of course, it took a day or two, and we had to sleep over on the train. What a wonder! This thing called a berth folded down out of the ceiling, and we children could crawl up and sleep in it as we were rocked by the gentle movement of the train. We got to eat elegant suppers in a dining car on what I thought were fine china and glassware. There were waiters and porters and conductors to serve us, and it was a marvelous adventure.

Another glory about train rides was watching America unfold in front of my eyes. There were countless cities and towns we passed through, all different and yet the same. There were small and massive farms, great rivers and small ones. Tremendous forests loomed and small woods skirted the rails. It was quite an education as countless telephone poles flew past my window. At night, I would wonder at all the little houses and what lives were being lived in them; what friends I might make; what dinners I might eat and what beds I might sleep in.

Every Christmas, the Lionel train set came out of its hiding place in the linen closet and was put up under the tree where we children would play with it for hours. Around and around we made it go, tooting its little whistle and chugging its little wheels. Each little car was a replica of a big one, and we could have circled the globe at least twice with our play journeys by the time Mama finally put the beat-up old train out at a garage sale where it went for less than $10.

As I grew older, I recall singing train songs in school. They were the songs of hobos and catastrophes. There was Casey Jones, that brave engineer who rode into history as his train plowed headlong into another. And who could forget poor old John Henry, the steel drivin' man who died from driving steel spikes into the rails so that trains could ride on them? There were songs about "The City of New Orleans" and "I've Been Workin' on the Railroad," and all of them flash through my nearly sleeping brain when the bedroom window is open and the sounds of the train yard seep through the curtains. Once again the magic of trains carries me away. I can almost feel the jostling motion that once carried me off to sleep. I can hear that "lonesome whistle blow," and very soon I am gone.

Life and Losing and a Friend Called Dobie

As I approach the half-century mark of my existence, I have come to realize that life is indeed a strange, mysterious thing. It can be a thrill-ride a minute or a deadly-dull crawl through time. In any case, life is short. It needs to be quickly appreciated and then, tenderly savored.

My first most challenging lesson in life came when my best friend Marguerite moved away to Tampa. It was so sad to watch as her family's Ford Falcon drove down the road and out of my life. The next lesson came in high school when my first real boyfriend, Bill, moved to Massachusetts our junior year before we even got to go to the prom; but one of the hardest lessons came when a neighbor of mine, Dobie, died at the age of thirty-four.

Before we even knew Dobie was ill, I was thirty-two and beginning to feel the "over the hill" pangs of not being a kid anymore. I was "getting so old," I complained to anyone who would listen. I had just gone back to teaching after having been on a two-year maternity leave, and I felt constantly stressed by my job and the demands of a family with two young children. I guess all my co-workers felt similar stresses because they would nod and agree with my every complaint and then add some of their own.

It was about this time that Dobie's thirty-four years began to come to an end. Here she was, a vibrant mother of two, just like me. She was an extraordinary person whose very presence in a room commanded your attention and made you glad she had come. Her laugh even now fills my heart when I think of her. All who loved her watched as cancer slowly took her strength, but never her love of life. It seemed that no matter how bleak the situation, Dobie always had a joke to tell or a funny anecdote about what either of her sons had done.

One of her most endearing qualities was her incredible industry. She was always making one of a jillion projects. I went to visit her once and found her surrounded by countless scraps of cloth, glue pots, sticks, wires and the twenty or so kitchen witches she had made for the neighborhood bazaar. It was quite a picture.

One day near the end, as Dobie clung desperately to life so that she could have a few more days with her young sons, I realized that I was exceedingly immature to have ever complained about getting old. After all, unlike Dobie, I would get the joy of continuing in life with my family. I would get to watch my children stumble and fall and get up again and again. Sure, I would get to "enjoy" the teen years and the "I-hate-everything-about-you-Mom" phase; but I would also get to see band concerts and senior pictures and glorious graduations and more. I would at least get to see my children grown and on their way in this world, and one can only do that if he or she grows old.

Whenever our family times are painful and hard, I just remember Dobie's short, precious life and how she would have given a king's ransom to have what I have—life and husband and family. Then I stop feeling sorry for myself and get on with the business of appreciating all that I have.

Gather Ye Rosebuds
To Anne "Dobie" Michael

fill your aprons
with the goodbyes

of lovers
and babies

and lives
put them

into your cookies
and sewing baskets

roll them out
in your pies

knead them
into your loaves

because
you never know

when you'll miss
that one farewell

you never saw
coming

Acknowledgements

"Wind Chimes" appeared in *The Florida Times Union* on May 19, 1996. It also appeared in "Porch Tales" on the website www.southernscribe.com.

"Barefoot" appeared in the fall edition of *Rough Draft* in 1997.

"Memory, Mountains, and Marguerite" appeared on the website www.southernscribe.com.

"Nature of the Beast" and "Overgrown" appeared in *Paws and Tales* Volume 1 in 1998.

"Key West Cats" appeared in *The Florida Times Union* on December 9, 2001.

"Thanksgiving at Ernest Hemingway's House" won 2nd place of the 2004 Douglas Freel Poetry Contest sponsored by Florida Community College at Jacksonville. It also appeared in *Key West: A Collection* published by White Fish Press in 2001.

"Encountering the Feminine" appeared in *Voices International* Volume 27, Number 1 in 1992.

"Mama's House," "Women I Have Loved," and "Duchess" appeared in *International Poetry Review*, Volume XVII, Number 2 in Fall of 1991.

"Mama's Garden" appeared in *The Florida Times Union* in August 5, 1995.

"Eve's Garden" appeared in *Skylark*, Fall issue of 1994.

"Neenie's Chess Pie and Recipe" appeared in *What's Cooking?* Volume 1 Issue 2 in 2000.

"Lady Food" appeared in *The Artful Mind* in 1998.

"Sleeping with Bears" appeared in *Sublime Odyssey* Issue #2 in 1995.

"Unremembered Acts" appeared in *Messages from the Heart*, Volume 3, Issue 2, Spring 1995.

"Man by Van Gogh" appeared in *The Key West Review*, Volume 2, Numbers 1 and 2, Fall and Winter 1989.

"Wonderment" appeared in *The Florida Times Union* on March 4, 1996.

"Casey's Touch appeared in the *2001 Emily Dickinson Award Anthology* published in 2002.

"New Beginnings and the Empty Nest" appeared in The *Florida Times Union* on October 7, 1997.

"Quilting Harvest" appeared in *Olden Times*, Volume 1, Number 2, Summer of 1996.

"The Magnolia Tree and Me" appeared in the anthology *Tree Stories* published by Sunshine Press Publications in 2002.

"The Christmas Cactus" appeared in *The Florida Times Union* on December 21, 1996. It also has appeared on the website www.southernscribe.com.

About the Author

Dorothy K. Fletcher has taught English for over thirty years in Jacksonville, Florida. Along with teaching, writing is her passion. Her poetry has appeared in over 80 literary magazines including *Kalliope* and *Key West Review*. More than 20 of her articles have appeared in *The Florida Times Union*, and she has also had essays and articles published in *Coastal Traveling Magazine*, *Small Press Review*, *Florida English Journal*, *Folio Weekly*, and *Jacksonville Magazine*.

Her children's book *The Week of Dream Horses* was published in 1984 and in October, 2004, she published her first novel, *The Cruelest Months*, a book about a first year teacher's trials and tribulations in an inner city school that was based upon her experiences in the classroom. *The Cruelest Months* has touched a chord with educators and all who care about kids.